MIRAGE...

OF UNREAL MUSINGS AND EVERYDAY LIFE...

LAKSHMY NAIR

ISBN 979-888606608-1

Pramod

Dhananjay

Azaad

Akira….

……This book is for you guys…

Contents

Preface

FROM THE POET'S DESK…

"Mirage: Of Unreal Musings and Everyday Life" is a collection of 21 poems, including 8 Haiku Poems and 13 long poems, that are the poet's musings on life and myriad human emotions. The poems touch upon varying themes including love, the pain of loss, and ironies of life. Some of them will bring a smile to your face and some others will leave you lost in reflection. And maybe… just maybe, some of them would make you want to go back and hug those loved ones and let them know that they mean the world to you…Happy reading!

• Lakshmy Nair

Acknowledgements

The book of my unreal musings has finally become a reality in this very real world! While I am elated by this incredible fact, I also realize that none of this would have been possible if not for the unflinching support and love from some of my best people.

Thank you, Pramod P B, my dear husband, for being the rock behind this wild woman, so that she could finally gather the courage to pen down her wild thoughts and let the world hold them and read them. Thank you, my boys, Dhananjay and Azaad, for patiently putting up with Mumma's long working hours and being your best selves all throughout. Thank you to all my dear friends who read through my writings and gave honest feedbacks, which helped me evolve and better myself as a writer. Last, but not the least, thank you Lord Almighty, for holding my hand through all ups and downs in life. For me, traversing through them definitely helped put into perspective the mirage that life is...

My list of gratitude would never be complete without thanking each one of my dear readers for loving my work, supporting, and encouraging me. You'all inspire me to write more! Thank you from the bottom of my heart. Love to each one of you.

1. The Tragic love story.

He gifted a rose.
Stung by the bee in the rose,
She broke up in wrath!

2. Old Age

It was the date night,
Planned after long forty years.
Alas! They forgot!

3. The Mosquito

He hummed a sweet note,
In her lovely little ears.
Till the time she clapped.

4. Festering Wounds

Tidying her closet,
She chanced on the scarf of love.
And the pain returned.

5. The Pandemic

She gifted herself
A glossy red lipstick, but,
Fate gifted a mask!

6. Still Life

Flowers in the vase,
Looked pretty, but still and dull;
Like her, in her bed.

7. Apology

Waves washed her tired feet.
To atone for the vile sin,
Of killing her child.

8. Siesta

The cat purred softly,
Sitting on old Grandma's lap.
She snored in her nap.

9. The Cacophony

Around her was a cacophony of deafening clamor.
It was the world outside with all the hustle and glamour.
She wished always,
For a change of ways.
For a quieter place.
With a slower pace.
But the dissonance outside was meant to be.
Her dissent, just made her a deviant lass.
The din outside was rising each day,
Into an impregnable fort of torment and dismay.
She darted back to a zone of her own,
A peaceful place with happiness sown.
But with each step she took, her being shook!
For, the noise grew loud and clear,
Caterwauling right into her ear!
Behind her back, she closed the door,
Bolted the glass panes across the floor.
And then she ran to peep by the window sill,
But alas! the noise grew louder still.
And then she knew all at once,
The genesis of the deafening cacophony.
It was not around her,

MIRAGE...

It was not behind her.
It was within her!
Inside her soul and substance.

****

10. Abandoned

Stinking.
Cold.
Fraught with flies.
The trash dump is her home.
Her home, where she lives,
with a broken heart and broken life,
After they dumped her in the pile.
Her life was a dream,
In an opulent home,
Petted by loving hand,.
Until the day she was dumped.
Sad and scared,
In the pile of trash.
Stinking.
Cold.
Fraught with flies.
She missed the warmth.
She missed the cuddle.
She missed being hugged,
And kissed with love.
She missed her teddy she curled up with,
In her homey kennel,

Snug as a bug.
Did she hear a baby cry?
A weak wail from the pile of trash?
Ears pricked, she ran,
To the find a little angel.
Dumped to die.
In the pile of trash.
Stinking.
Cold.
Fraught with flies.
She loved the warmth.
The cozy cuddle.
The hug,
And the lick of love.
Her motherly fondness,
Oozed from her teats,
Moistening the tiny dry lips.
As the dusk set in,
She curled up with the little one.
Glad and serene.
Amidst the pile of trash.
Still Stinking.
Still Cold.
And still fraught with flies.

****

11. Eyes

It is said, eyes are the windows to soul,
That they bespeak undivulged thoughts in whole.
Amazed,
I sat and gazed.
I gazed at a pair of dark brown eyes.
Neath' them were thoughts in disguise.
But alas!
I tried to delve into them in vain,
For the dark brown eyes looked away in disdain!
I gazed into a pair of ocean blue.
With this soul, I hoped for a rendezvous.
But alas!
Like the water in the abyssal zone,
The eyes had a cold undertone.
Perplexed, I foraged a pair of aqua green,
And met with pretentious emotions devoid of sheen.
I searched and searched with weary eyes,
But now I knew it was all, but lies.
It is said, eyes are the windows to soul.
That they bespeak undivulged thoughts in whole.
Dazed,
I sat and gazed.

MIRAGE...

I gazed at the twinkling eyes of a baby girl.
And lo! My heart made a joyous twirl.
For her eyes beamed with love so pure,
They were windows to her soul for sure.
Oh! Let me behold this sight for a little while,
With time those eyes will begin to beguile.

****

12. It's OK

They said,
Feeling sad is ok.
Feeling bad is ok.
But you have to share,
Because we care.
So, I share.
Because they are there.
But when I shared,
No one cared.
Now they are here,
By my pyre.
Feeling sad for me.
Feeling bad for me.
Wishing that they cared,
When I shared.
You can be someone's sunshine.
Save a mind quite labyrinthine.
All you have to do is take stock,
And walk the talk.
All you have to do is be there,
When they finally share.

****

13. The Chrysalis

The warmth of the cocoon was comforting,
Yet she still was in pain, yes, she was hurting.
Reminiscences from the past,
Were festering wounds that left her aghast.
She coiled deeper in her cocoon,
Hoping against hope for solace soon.
She was once a happy caterpillar,
For whom the world was an intriguing thriller!
But her beautiful world fell apart, hard and bad,
The ravage draining away the hopes she had.
Despised for being the cringy worm,
She was a delicious meal for some.
Scared and scarred by the ways of the world,
She climbed into her little cocoon and curled.
She fought her demons all this while,
And now as a Chrysalis she had a smile.
For now, she realized the secret of peace,
And that was to digest all that was her with ease.
Slowly, painfully she transformed each day,
One inch at a time, but knowing herself all the way.
Until that day when she felt something change.
She wondered if the worm had a soul exchange.

She no longer wanted to hang on the tree.
She wanted to fly over the hills and the sea.
She no longer wanted to devour the leaves.
Sweetness of nectar was what her mind conceived.
And so, she flew over the hills,
Accepting that the world despises her will.
But now she longer cared...
As she flew over the clear blue lake,
She saw herself and perceived her bosom quake.
The bright colors of her wings shone in the sun.
Flowers admired her, disregarding bygones.
Now, her beauty was a psychedelic vision,
Spreading colors and grace she never could envision.
The beautiful butterfly stood mesmerized by the lake,
Loving her being solely for her soul's sake.
Cherishing those dark days in the cocoon,
For, it was the pain that made her this beauty so soon.

****

14. The Painting

On the wall of her room, hung the painting.
Of the man and his beloved.
She gazed at it all day and all night,
Lying on her bed,
That emanates myriad odors, myriad memories...
And every time she gazed,
She was mesmerized...
The beloved lay on his lap,
And the man kissed her lips,
The fire of passion burning in their eyes!
In a reverie, she travelled to their world,
He was a sculptor and she was his muse.
And together they created an enchanting world,
where they shared their love and spirit for life.
She watched him caress her hair,
Hug her tight, she knows he cares.
She watched them share laughs,
Lost in the eyes of their better halves.
She watched them fight the world for their love,
A world that despised their forbidden love.
Until one day,
Love did triumph, but in death.

The beloved lay on his lap.
And the man kissed her lips,
Licking the last drop of poisonous froth,
That spilled off her mouth.
The fire of passion burning in their eyes!
And before the deadly poison took their lives,
The time stood still within the canvas, amidst the motley of
colors...
She lay on her bed gazing at the wall,
At the man and her beloved and their kiss of love,
Lost in her reverie world of unreal love.
And then...
Reality knocked.
Jolted out from her reverie world,
She opened the door and in came a man.
With a different odor,
To leave behind a different memory.
He hid his face inside her hair,
Eyes burning with ravenous lust.
As she hugged him tight,
The bed creaked under their weight.
But she was still gazing at the wall,
Marveling at the passion of love,
That burned in the eyes,
Of the man and his beloved.
A passion she searched for in vain,
In the eyes of the men who came to her.

All she found in her men,
Were Myriad odors...
That left Myriad memories ...

****

15. Birth

The darkness has a comforting charm,

It's a microcosmic realm of an obscure macrocosm.

For how long I lay, I know not.

My eyes shut tight,

Blocking every iota of light.

I hear them say,

There is indeed a bright world beyond the tunnel of murk,

But my mind trepidate for the unknowns that lurk.

All I wish is to curl up in the darkness,

Soaking in its warmth and tranquil happiness.

But then I move!

swiftly before I knew!

Towards the unknown, to the mystique light.

My qualms and fear give way to cheer,

And I slide with glee to embrace the new light.

An eternity later…

I open my eyes.

The ever-familiar darkness has vanished to oblivion.

I find myself in a different realm.

Snug and warm, in a caring arm.

A pair of beautiful loving eyes look down at me,

Hailing me into the world of light.

16. Crushed

The little girl was a happy butterfly,
Who did not know how to be cunning and sly.
She loved the beauty of her world,
And her people were but all her world.
She loved to hop around him all the time,
He told her stories and sang her rhyme.
More than common blood, he was a friend,
Whom she believed she can always depend.
Until one day...
She realized his fingers ran astray,
All over her when they went away,
Into the woods.
When no one watched.
She ran back wiping big drops of tears,
Jerking out of her eyes with unknown fears.
She fell on her mother's lap, crying in anguish,
And told the story of a character so greyish.
After a silence for eternity,
Came the warning to shut up with certainty.
It was then that the little butterfly lost her trust,
Since then, all she knew was a sense of disgust.

****

17. First Love

T'was an accident,
The locking of their eyes.
In the crowded bus.
She was a shy girl still blooming,
who found his intense gaze sweeping.
After brief moments of an unknown emotion,
That showed her glimpses of a new found devotion,
She looked away.
From those deep-set eyes,
That took her by surprise.
In the days to come,
T'was not an accident.
The locking of their eyes,
In the crowded bus.
They waited for the scintillating journey of love,
When unknown feelings interwove.
Their eyes indeed did essay,
All that words could never convey.
Neither did she know his name.
Nor did he know her home.
Still one day,
She found him standing at her door.

With a group of lads, out on their chore.

She talked to them as if in a trance.

Her eyes fixated in those deep-set eyes, full of romance.

Their eyes indeed did essay,

All that words could never convey.

Soon t'was time for her to leave.

Though she was not deceptive.

There were dreams to chase,

And a living to make.

In the sands of time, he became a memory,

His deep-set eyes, a forgotten story.

Many summers later,

Many springs after,

She chanced upon those pair of deep-set eyes.

That took her by surprise.

For a moment,

Their eyes indeed did essay,

All that words could never convey.

But alas,

By then, she had to look away.

For, she was already taken away.

By someone whose words could convey

All that his deep-set eyes could essay.

****

18. Waiting for the rain

As crimson breaks in the morning sky,
Off to the wild blue yonder she would fly.
For there are mouths to feed in her little nest,
And for them she needs to bring home the best.
She was the hornbill waiting for the rain,
She wanted a life without all the pain.
She knew her nest was a happy place,
Where love of her chicks filled her hollow space.
Yet she wished, there was more to life,
To soar like the eagle, away from the trife.
Yearning for the magical raindrops of fervor,
To fill her days with rhapsodic joy to savor.
She was the hornbill waiting for the rain...
A lone eagle sat watching from the pinnacle,
For her the little nest was nothing but a miracle.
A marvel of gaiety and cozy amore,
From where she would no longer wish to soar.
She wished for the life of a hornbill,
Waiting for the rain, than fighting all the storms.
But life moves on with vicious bizarre norms,
The pastures beyond are always greener still...

****

19. Ashes

Every time the fire burnt,
The world cowered, for that's what they've learnt.
But she remained hopeful.
For the fire was her harbinger of times cheerful.
She was the phoenix,
With beautiful colorful wings.
The one with alluring feathers,
Desired much across all the weathers.
Every time she rose from the ashes,
Spreading her glowing wings,
She was hailed the queen in fire flashes,
And in her praise, the cosmos sings.
But this time as she burnt, she turned reflective.
The vicious circle of rebirths all of a sudden seemed deceptive.
As the fire slowly burnt out, into a grey glowing hill,
She did not, from the ashes, majestically rise up with her will.
Instead...
She pulled over the blanket of ashes,
Closing her eyes in eternal slumber.
Becoming the mystical mythical bird...
That went back to her ashes and ember...

****

20. Yearning

I stood by the window,
Watching sun set across the meadow.
The sky was a dusky beauty,
Waiting for her beloved so naughty.
But is not her beauty so peripheral?
For everything around is so ephemeral.
Ephemeral dreams,
Born out of ephemeral whims.
Ephemeral joys,
Gifts of an ephemeral choice.
Ephemeral sorrows,
Scarring the soul with ephemeral hollows.
Ephemeral days, full of strife,
And Ephemeral nights, sans any life.
Like the dusky sky, the beauty,
I wait for you, my beloved so naughty.
For my love for you is not peripheral.
The pain of separation is not ephemeral.
I stand by the window,
Watching sun sets.
The ephemeral moments,
Before the night sets.

Longing to hide my face,
In your warm embrace.
Wishing, the yearning was ephemeral.
But dear me!
I am lost in eternal wait...
I am lost in eternal love...

****

21. Celebrations

She stood by the window, brumal winds making her quiver.
Her eyes darted around the lights, colors and the shimmer.
Very many lives, celebrating their quiddities, caged in an illusory
abode of abundance!
Once a little girl loved her walk to school,
Past the tattered thatched huts with tiny little doors.
Her inquisitive eyes scanning every face, searching for stories to
read.
Very many lives, milled around, laboring for a paltry survival.
Yet they celebrated life, as belly laughs and merry banters rang
amidst the din!
She stood by the window, gazing at the darkness and the colors
beyond,
Marveling at the thought of two celebrations with different
meanings.
One of sequestered existence and another of blithe freedom!

About The Author

Lakshmy Nair is a banker turned writer, a finance professional, and an entrepreneur. She was born and raised in a small village in Thiruvananthapuram, the capital of the beautiful state of Kerala in India. Lakshmy worked as an analyst, as a teacher, and then as a banker for 10 years, before finally settling down to live her passion of being a writer. If she isn't spending time writing, you can almost always find her managing her content writing business at Qualitas Engrafo (OPC) Pvt Ltd, researching and managing her investment portfolio, bustling around her family, or dancing Bharatanatyam. Lakshmy currently lives in Nagpur, with her husband Pramod P B, her two sons, Dhananjay and Azaad, and her adorable golden retriever, Akira. You can reach out to her by mailing to lakshmypramod@gmail.com.